Bible
Doctrine
Workbook

T0308393

Bible Doctrine Workbook

Study Questions and Practical Exercises for Learning the
Essential Teachings of the Christian Faith

WAYNE GRUDEM
BRIANNA SMITH
ERIK THOENNES

ZONDERVAN
ACADEMIC

ZONDERVAN ACADEMIC

Bible Doctrine Workbook
Copyright © 2022 by Wayne Grudem

Requests for information should be addressed to:
Zondervan, *3900 Sparks Dr. SE, Grand Rapids, Michigan 49546*

Zondervan titles may be purchased in bulk for educational, business, fundraising, or sales promotional use. For information, please email SpecialMarkets@Zondervan.com.

ISBN 978-0-310-13617-0 (softcover)

ISBN 978-0-310-13618-7 (ebook)

Cover design: Brand Navigation
Cover photos: © Janet Worne / Alamy Stock Photo
Interior design: Kait Lamphere

Contents

PART 5: The Doctrine of the Application of Redemption

PART 6: The Doctrine of the Church

PART 7: The Doctrine of the Future

A Note to the Reader

Wayne Grudem's *Bible Doctrine* is an incredibly helpful resource for those looking to learn more about the foundations of their faith as the Bible teaches them. In our own lives, we have found that such resources can help us greatly as we seek to know God better and worship him more fully. Ultimately, there is no better place to turn for answers than God's Word, and we pray that this workbook will help you dig deep into God's Word even as it helps you learn from Dr. Grudem's work. Within the workbook, you will find questions regarding the main points of each chapter that will help you contemplate and process what you have learned. After each section, there is also a short quiz that you can use as a tool to test what you have retained from each chapter. Whether you use this workbook alone or with others, we hope and pray that the Lord will use it to promote learning, rich discussion, and conversations centered on biblical truths. Along with Dr. Grudem, our main goals are that this resource will be used by the Lord to inform his people, strengthen their faith, deepen personal relationships with him, and increase his glory on earth. To him alone be the glory for this and all things!

WITH GRATITUDE,
Brianna Smith and Erik Thoennes

CHAPTER 1

Introduction to Systematic Theology

OPENING PRAYER

Lord, open my heart and my mind so that I may discern what is true. Thank you that you are a God of order, clarity, and reason, and that your Word and your ways make sense and lead to life. Teach me from the study of your Word, and allow your Spirit to transform my life through this study for your glory and honor. Amen.

CHAPTER REVIEW

1. What is systematic theology? Restate the definition in *Biblical Doctrine* in your own words.

2. How is systematic theology different from biblical, historical, and philosophical theology?

3. Draw a line to connect each following question with the proper category of study:

What does the Bible teach
about prayer?

Biblical theology

Old Testament theology

How does the teaching regarding
prayer develop in the Bible?

Historical theology

What does Paul teach about
prayer?

New Testament theology

Systematic theology

What do the Psalms teach
about prayer?

How did fourth century
Christians pray?

4. Why does systematic theology use terms that are not found in Scripture?

5. Fill in the blank: The adjective *systematic* in systematic _____ should be understood to mean something like "_____ organized by _____."

6. According to Dr. Grudem, the opposite of "systematic" in systematic theology is: (circle the correct answer/s)

    a. Randomly arranged
    b. Clear
    c. Disorganized
    d. Ordered

7. What is the difference between how most Christians do systematic theology and the more formal study of systematic theology found in this book?

8. Why should someone change their mind regarding a particular doctrine? Circle the correct answer.

    a. A teacher/pastor/mentor told them to
    b. Based upon a particularly compelling sermon or argument
    c. Because the Bible teaches differently than their former belief
    d. Based solely upon a dream or vision

9. How does Dr. Grudem define doctrine? Rewrite the definition in your own words.

10. What is the distinction between a major and minor doctrine? Give a few examples of each.

11. How does systematic theology help us to address future controversies?

12. What is the relationship between spiritual growth and systematic theology?

BIBLICAL ENGAGEMENT

13. Dr. Grudem says that "most Christians actually do systematic theology many times a week" as they make statements about what the Bible says. What are some true systematic statements about the Bible that you know or regularly say? For example, "The Bible says that Jesus is coming again." List references to back up your statements.

14. In Psalm 119:18, the psalmist prays, "Open my eyes, that I may behold wondrous things out of your law." Why might the psalmist feel he must pray this way as he engages with God's Word? Feel free to use other passages to support your answer.

PERSONAL APPLICATION

15. Have you considered what God wants you to *believe* and to *know*? How can you grow your understanding of what these things might be?

16. What kind of personal value is there in studying systematic theology? Have you experienced such value in your own life?

17. Considering the information found in this chapter, how would you like to grow in your own study or practice of systematic theology? Spend some time asking the Lord to help you engage in this practice.

18. Which doctrine discussed in this book are you most interested in learning more about? Write out some questions you hope are addressed in this book.

19. Having read the reasons Christians should study theology, do you find any reason particularly compelling or convicting? Invite the Spirit to work in your heart based on this reflection.

20. Dr. Grudem states we should study systematic theology with prayer, humility, reason, help from others, by collecting and understanding all the relevant passages of Scripture, and with rejoicing and praise. Which of these do you currently find most difficult to practice? Prayerfully brainstorm some ways to grow in this area.

PART 1

The Doctrine of the Word of God

CHAPTER 2

The Authority and Inerrancy of the Bible

OPENING PRAYER

Lord, teach me to submit to your Word as my authority because it comes from you (Ps. 119:4) and to know that "every word of God proves true" (Prov. 30:5). You are perfect, so of course your words are perfect also. Your Word brings comfort but also conviction; it brings peace but also exposes our foolishness and sin. You are good, and all you command is good and life giving. Please give me a reverence for your Word so that the knowledge I gain will lead to my obedience to it. Amen.

CHAPTER REVIEW

1. What does Grudem state as the four characteristics of Scripture?

a.

b.

c.

d.

2. Define the *authority of Scripture*:

3. What does the Bible claim when it uses phrases like "Thus says the LORD"?

4. Describe the relationship between God and the prophets in the Bible.

5. *Breathing* in 2 Timothy 3:16 is a metaphor for:

    a. Surviving
    b. Speaking
    c. Swimming
    d. Stirring

6. True / False: One can say "God said" of the words in the Old Testament. Explain your answer.

7. Why is the Bible more persuasive than other religious books?

8. The process of persuasion is best likened to what shape according to Grudem?

    a. Circle
    b. Triangle
    c. Spiral
    d. Cone

9. Fill in the blanks: To disbelieve or _____ any word of Scripture is to disbelieve or _____ God.

10. What is the difference between saying God's words are true and that God's Word is truth?

11. Define *inerrancy*.

BIBLICAL ENGAGEMENT

12. What does 2 Timothy 3:16 teach us about God's Word? Write out factual statements that we can discern from this verse.

13. Grudem mentions several different means of communication from God to the biblical authors from Luke 1:1–3; John 14:26; Hebrews 1:1; and Revelation 2:1, 8, 12. What do each of these communicate about how God interacts with his people?

PERSONAL APPLICATION

14. Do you engage with Scripture like it is the very Word of God? Ask God to help you to grow in your trust that reading Scripture is reading his Word.

15. How does confidence in the inerrancy of the Bible help you engage the text of the Bible devotionally?

CHAPTER 3

The Clarity, Necessity, and Sufficiency of the Bible

OPENING PRAYER

Lord, your Word is clear because you love to lead your children into understanding and not confusion. Without your Word we would be helpless in our quest to know you and your ways. Help me to trust that it has everything I need for a godly life (2 Peter 1:3). Please "give me understanding, that I may keep your law and observe it with my whole heart" (Ps. 119:34). Amen.

CHAPTER REVIEW

1. Define the *clarity of Scripture* in your own words.

2. True / False: The Bible is too difficult for everyone to understand.

3. Complete the following chart of the requirements for understanding Scripture rightly:

Requirement	Definition (in your own words)	Scriptural Evidence
Time		
Effort		
The use of ordinary means		
A willingness to obey		
The help of the Holy Spirit		
A humble recognition that our understanding is imperfect		

4. Explain why there is always more that we can learn from Scripture.

5. What is the role of scholars considering the doctrine of the clarity of Scripture?

6. Define the *necessity of Scripture*.

7. True / False: The Bible is necessary for salvation. Explain.

8. Fill in the blanks: The _____ of Scripture means that Scripture contained _____ the words of God he intended his people to have at each _____ of redemptive history, and that it now contains _____ we need God to tell us for salvation, for _____ him perfectly, and for obeying him _____.

BIBLICAL ENGAGEMENT

9. In Deuteronomy 6:6–7, the Bible says, "These words that I command you today shall be on your heart. You shall teach them diligently to your children, and shall talk of them when you sit in your house, and when you walk by the way, and when you lie down, and when you rise." What do you think these statements communicate about how we should engage with Scripture? How might this verse get rewritten for the modern reader?

10. What does Romans 1:19–21 communicate about the knowability of God apart from Scripture? What kinds of things can those who do not know Scripture know about God?

PERSONAL APPLICATION

11. As you consider the seven qualifications/requirements for understanding Scripture rightly, which do you have the most trouble with? Ask the Lord to help you grow in this area.

12. How does thinking about the necessity of Scripture help you think about evangelism and missions? Do you feel called to engage in any particular way in the advancement of the gospel among the nations?

13. Do you think of spending time in Scripture as helping you in your walk with the Lord? How has the Bible worked to "make you wise for salvation" (2 Tim. 3:15)?

14. What role does the Bible play in your assessment of what you should do in any given situation? Do you allow it to be sufficient, or do you primarily seek assurance from other sources?

Part 1 Review Quiz

1. True / False: The Bible claims that all its words are God's words.

2. Our conviction that the words of the Bible are God's words comes:

    a. When we become Christians
    b. With a clear understanding of the gospel
    c. By the power of the Holy Spirit

3. Fill in the blank: To disbelieve or disobey any word of Scripture is to disbelieve or disobey _____.

4. The _____ of Scripture means that Scripture in the original manuscripts does not affirm anything which is contrary to fact.

    a. Trustworthiness
    b. Truthfulness
    c. Inerrancy
    d. Completion

5. True / False: One can say "God said" of the words in the Old Testament.

6. Which of the following is not one of the four characteristics of Scripture discussed in *Bible Doctrine*?

    a. Clarity
    b. Necessity
    c. Accuracy
    d. Authority

7. True / False: People can know things about God apart from the Bible.

8. Breathing in 2 Timothy 3:16 is a metaphor for:

    a. Surviving
    b. Speaking
    c. Swimming
    d. Stirring

9. True / False: The Bible is too difficult for everyone to understand.

10. Match the following words to their definitions below:

    a. Clarity   c. Universalism
    b. Necessity   d. Sufficiency

_____ All people who ever lived will be saved.

_____ Scripture contained all the words of God he intended his people to have at each stage of redemptive history, and that it now contains everything we need God to tell us for salvation, for trusting him perfectly, and for obeying him perfectly.

_____ The Bible is written in such a way that is able to be understood.

_____ The Bible is essential for knowledge of the gospel, for maintaining spiritual life, and for certain knowledge of God's will.

PART 2

The Doctrine
of God

CHAPTER 4

The Character of God: "Incommunicable" Attributes

OPENING PRAYER

Lord, you are! You exist all by yourself, and you have always existed. What a joyful and amazing truth that even though you are infinite, you reveal yourself to us and you are knowable. Show me the beauty of your complex nature through your attributes. Please help me to know you more deeply as I ponder your character, and give me a healthy, holy fear of you. May I honor you with who I am and how I live. In your mighty, good name I pray. Amen.

CHAPTER REVIEW

1. How do we know that God exists?

   a.

   b.

2. True / False: It is possible to fully understand God.

3. Fill in the blanks: We can never _____ any of God's _____
completely or _____.

4. Define *communicable* and *incommunicable* as they relate to God's
attributes. Give examples of each.

5. Explain how some of God's attributes can be both communicable and
incommunicable (e.g., wisdom).

6. Match each attribute with its corresponding definition.

    a. Independence
    b. Unchangeableness
    c. Eternity
    d. Omnipresence

_____ God does not have size or spatial dimensions and is present at every point of space with his whole being, yet God acts differently in different places.

_____ God does not need us or the rest of creation for anything, yet we and the rest of creation glorify him and bring him joy.

_____ God has no beginning, end, or succession of moments in his own being, and he sees all time equally vividly, yet God sees events in time and acts in time.

_____ God is unchanging in his being, perfections, purposes, and promises, yet God does act and feel emotions, and he acts and feels differently in response to different situations.

BIBLICAL ENGAGEMENT

7. Read Genesis 1. What can we learn about God and his character from just this first chapter of Scripture?

8. Without looking at any references, list as many attributes/characteristics of God that you can think of that are addressed in Scripture. (For a fun challenge, try to list attributes from A-Z!) After making your list, use a Bible search engine online to find references for each attribute.

9. Pick one of God's incommunicable attributes and look it up in a Bible dictionary. In what ways did your understanding of the attribute change or deepen after reading the definition?

PERSONAL APPLICATION

10. Are you experiencing your inner awareness of God growing stronger and more distinct? Pray and ask God to help you increasingly know his existence is real and tangible in your life.

11. How might knowing the incommunicable attributes of God help you relate to him in prayer?

12. Which attribute of God are you especially grateful for after reading this chapter? Write a prayer thanking God for this aspect of his character.

CHAPTER 5

The "Communicable" Attributes of God

OPENING PRAYER

Lord, you are gracious, kind, loving, merciful, wise, patient, and good. Teach me to see you in the ways that I am like you, and continue to transform me to be more like you. Help me to learn to love everything about you, especially the things that are hard to easily like or understand. Help me, Father, to bear the fruit of the Spirit and to be conformed to the image of Christ in ways that give others a glimpse of who you are so that they will praise your holy name. Amen.

CHAPTER REVIEW

1. What are the five major categories of God's "communicable" attributes?

a.

b.

c.

d.

e.

2. Define *theophany.*

3. Fill in the blanks: God fully _____ himself and all things _____ and possible in one simple and _____ act.

4. Define God's love. How is this different from how the world normally talks about love?

5. How would God be far less good if he were not wrathful?

6. What is the distinction between God's secret will and his revealed will?

7. Define *blessedness*.

BIBLICAL ENGAGEMENT

8. Ephesians 5:1 says, "Be imitators of God, as beloved children." Pick three of God's communicable attributes and describe how each can be imitated by Christians in their daily lives.

PERSONAL APPLICATION

9. Which communicable attribute is hardest for you to reflect personally? Which communicable attribute is easiest for you to reflect?

10. How does the reality of God's omniscience bring you comfort as you face unknowns in your life?

11. Is it difficult for you to praise God for his wrath? What have you learned about God's wrath in this chapter that may help you see this attribute of God as good and right?

CHAPTER 6

The Trinity

OPENING PRAYER

Father, Son, and Holy Spirit, thank you for the unified diversity of your character. Help me to understand this mystery of yourself revealed in Scripture. Father, you sent your Son, and the Spirit brought about the incarnation and empowered Jesus to accomplish his work to redeem lost sinners. The gospel would not be the gospel if you were not who you are as the one God in three persons. Help me to grow in my understanding of the Trinity so that I can understand your redeeming work better as well. Amen.

CHAPTER REVIEW

1. Define the doctrine of the Trinity.

2. True / False: The word *trinity* is found in the Bible in a few places.

3. What are the three statements that summarize the biblical teaching on the Trinity?

a.

b.

c.

4. Explain a piece of evidence that points to the full divinity of each of the persons of the Trinity.

5. Beside each heresy, put the number corresponding to the statement about the Trinity it denies.

a. God is three persons   _____ Modalism
b. Each person is fully God   _____ Subordinationism
c. There is one God   _____ Tritheism
                                    _____ Arianism

6. Why is the doctrine of the Trinity so important?

7. Draw a line between the person of the Trinity and their role(s) in creation and redemption:

God the Father   Applies redemption

God the Son   Sustained God's presence in
                                            creation
God the Holy Spirit
                                            Carried out creative decrees
Accomplished redemption
                                            Planned redemption
Spoke creative words

8. Give a brief definition of the eternal generation of the Son in your own words.

9. True / False: The persons of the Trinity could easily switch roles in redemption.

10. Fill in the blanks: The pattern of Father-Son interaction in Scripture is one-directional, _____ the Father and _____ the Son.

11. Is it possible to understand the doctrine of the Trinity? Explain.

BIBLICAL ENGAGEMENT

12. Having read the biblical evidence on the Trinity from the Old and New Testaments, which passage or passages are most convincing or compelling to you?

13. In 1 Corinthians 12:12, Paul speaks of the church as "one body" with "many members." What are some examples of how the church reflects the image of the Trinitarian nature of God in this reality? How could your church grow in reflecting the image of God's unity and diversity?

PERSONAL APPLICATION

14. Can you think of an example of unity and diversity in your own life? How does knowing more about the doctrine of the Trinity help you value those instances of human unity and diversity more?

15. How do you relate to each person of the Trinity? Is there one whom you tend to focus on or one whom you often neglect? Ask God to help you relate to him rightly, appreciating both the equality and distinctions of the persons of the Trinity.

CHAPTER 7

Creation

OPENING PRAYER

Almighty Maker of heaven and earth, all of creation declares your glory. Worship is the only right response when we ponder the work of your hands. Teach me to appreciate your creativity, and let that which you have created point me to greater worship of you. Amen.

CHAPTER REVIEW

1. Define the *doctrine of creation*:

2. *Ex nihilo* is Latin for (circle the correct answer):

    a. out of something
    b. by word
    c. without error
    d. out of nothing

3. Fill in the blanks: Creation is _____ from God yet always _____ on God.

4. Define both *transcendent* and *immanent*.

5. How does the biblical account of creation refute pantheism?

6. Creation primarily shows us:

    a. God's care for his people
    b. God's glory
    c. God's creativity
    d. God's specificity

7. True / False: When all the facts are rightly understood, there will inevitably be conflict between Scripture and natural science.

8. What are some of the different ways the word "evolution" is used?

9. Define *theistic evolution*. How is it different from the biblical teaching regarding creation?

10. True / False: There are gaps in biblical genealogies.

11. Explain the day-age or "concordist" view. How is its approach different from the literary framework view?

BIBLICAL ENGAGEMENT

12. Read the creation account in Genesis 1–2. What are some things that you learn about God's act of creation, particularly of Adam and Eve? List your observations below.

13. Reread Genesis 1. Which aspects of the chapter support the young earth view? Which aspects support the old earth view?

PERSONAL APPLICATION

14. In what ways do you reflect the creative nature of God in your own life? Thank God for this way to praise him!

15. Has the theory of evolution posed an issue for you in regard to your belief in a creator God? How has this chapter helped you in your faith in the teaching of the Bible regarding creation?

16. How should a right understanding of creation help your worship of God?

CHAPTER 8

God's Providence

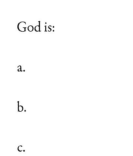

OPENING PRAYER

Lord, thank you for your sustaining control over all things in this world. Help me to see your hand at work and worship you more fully through this knowledge. Nothing happens outside of your wise, powerful, guiding hand. Help me to understand all that happens, even sin and evil, as part of your sovereign wisdom, and as a result may I grow in peace, gratitude, and hope. In Jesus's name I pray. Amen.

CHAPTER REVIEW

1. Define *providence*:

God is:

a.

b.

c.

2. True / False: God's providence provides a basis for science. Explain.

3. Fill in the blanks: God _____ with created things in every _____, directing their distinctive _____ to cause them to act as they do.

4. Explain God's work of concurrence in your own words.

5. Who bears the moral blame for evil actions?

6. True / False: Everything that is right for God to do is right for humans to do.

7. Define the following terms:

   a. *Libertarian free will*:

   b. *Freedom of inclination*:

c. Compare and contrast the two:

8. Does God's providence remove our responsibility to act? Explain.

9. What is one very significant means of ours that God has ordained to bring about results in this world? (Circle the correct answer.)

Sin   *Feats of strength*   *Prayer*   *Faith*   *Wisdom*

10. Describe the Arminian view of God's providence.

11. What are the main differences between the Calvinist and Arminian views?

12. Describe the middle-knowledge or Molinist view.

BIBLICAL ENGAGEMENT

13. Complete the verse: Genesis 50:20, "You meant evil against me, but God. . . ." How does the story of Joseph show us God's relationship to evil? Give examples.

PERSONAL APPLICATION

14. How does the knowledge of God's work of concurrence change your perspective on ordinary happenings, like getting food for lunch? How can you practice worshipful wonder at God's providential work in your life?

15. Job, in the midst of an incredible season of suffering, states with faith the following in Job 1:21: "The LORD gave, and the LORD has taken away; blessed be the name of the LORD." Have you experienced a time in your life in which you were able to make a similar statement of faith in the midst of suffering? Ask God to increase your faith in his goodness in the midst of all things.

16. In what areas of your life do you struggle to trust in God's providence? Pray and ask the Lord to help you see his providential hand in these areas.

CHAPTER 9

Prayer

OPENING PRAYER

Lord, what a great and awesome privilege to come into your presence in prayer. I know that this is only possible because of the finished work of Christ. Please help me to be a more prayerful person and rehearse the gospel every time I enter into your presence. Give me the proper humility and confidence as I pray, and help me to more fully draw near to you. Amen.

CHAPTER REVIEW

1. Define *prayer*. How is this definition different from what others might see prayer as?

2. Fill in the blanks: Prayer expresses our _____ in God and is a _____ whereby our trust in him can _____.

3. How does prayer affect our relationship with God?

4. True / False: Our prayers do not affect God's actions in the world. Explain.

5. Where do we enter with Christ as our mediator?

6. Praying *in Jesus' name* means praying (circle the correct answer):

    a. With "in Jesus' name" at the end
    b. Only words that Jesus would have prayed
    c. According to his character
    d. Repeatedly saying God's name throughout your prayer

7. Who are prayers normally directed to in Scripture? Does this exclude praying to other persons of the Trinity? Why or why not?

8. Fill in the blank: Knowledge of _____ is a tremendous help in prayer.

9. What does it mean to pray according to God's will?

10. How does obedience relate to prayer?

11. In what ways does a lack of forgiveness hinder prayer?

BIBLICAL ENGAGEMENT

12. Read the Lord's prayer in Matthew 6. What does this model of prayer teach us about prayer? What principles can we draw from this example?

13. Recount some examples of faithful prayers in Scripture. What do these examples show us about how we can pray to God?

PERSONAL APPLICATION

14. Assess your prayer life in light of this chapter. Is prayer something you engage in often? Why or why not?

15. How has this chapter changed your perspective on prayer? What information was new or especially meaningful for you?

16. Have you ever experienced having an unanswered prayer? How could you encourage yourself or others experiencing this with the knowledge you have gained from this chapter?

17. Finish your time in this chapter by writing out some praise and thanksgiving to God.

CHAPTER 10

Angels, Satan, and Demons

OPENING PRAYER

Lord of Hosts, I praise you that you have created your angelic messengers to worship and represent you as well as to minister to your people. We know that Satan prowls, seeking to destroy your work, but thank you that the powers of darkness will not ultimately triumph. Help me to be confident in the power of Christ over everything. Protect me by your Spirit as I seek to understand what your Word teaches about demons, and may your Spirit be the only power at work in my life. Amen.

CHAPTER REVIEW

1. Define *angels*. How does this definition differ from what you hear about angels in the world?

2. Circle all of the other terms used for angels in Scripture:

Holy ones	Ghosts	Invisible friend
Sons of God	Watchers	Deceased loved ones
Spirits	Thrones	Principalities
Ministering presence	Dominions	Authorities

3. Compare and contrast what we know about the cherubim and seraphim.

4. True / False: All angels carry the same rank in the spiritual realm.

5. What are some of the primary ways in which angels are distinct from humans?

6. Fill in the blank: Angels remind us that the _____ world is real.

7. Are angels always good and to be trusted? Explain your answer.

8. Define *demons*.

9. What does the name "Satan" mean?

    a. Prince of demons
    b. Adversary
    c. The serpent
    d. Evil angel

10. True / False: Sin originated with Satan.

11. Can demons read minds? Explain your answer.

12. Where does evil come from?

13. Why does Grudem prefer not to use the term *demon possessed*?

14. What kind of authority do believers have over demons?

BIBLICAL ENGAGEMENT

15. From memory, list some biblical accounts of angels and what they do. Then go back using a Bible software and add references to those accounts. Pick one and read through it. Were there any details about the angelic activity in the account that you had forgotten?

16. Why do Jesus and his followers have power over the demonic that has not been seen before? Explain this in light of the stages of the story of redemption set forth in the Bible.

PERSONAL APPLICATION

17. What personal beliefs or thoughts about angels do you need to adjust based on the teaching of scripture?

18. What personal beliefs or thoughts about demons do you need to adjust based on the teaching of scripture?

19. Do you think there are any areas in your life in which spiritual oppression might be happening? Pray and ask God to help you discern this, and then follow the steps outlined in this chapter to declare your authority in these areas.

Part 2 Review Quiz

1. True / False: All people have an inner sense of God.

2. The incomprehensibility of God means that:

    a. We can fully know God
    b. We can never fully understand God
    c. God is able to be truly known
    d. We are able to fully understand God

3. Match the following attributes with their definitions:

    a. Independence   d. Invisibility
    b. Unchangeableness   e. Truthfulness
    c. Omnipresence   f. Holiness

_____ God is separated from sin and devoted to seeking his own honor.

_____ God is unchanging in his being, perfections, purposes, and promises, yet God does act and feel emotions, and he acts and feels differently in response to different situations.

_____ God's total essence, all of his spiritual being, will never be able to be seen by us, yet God still shows himself to us through visible, created things.

_____ God does not need us or the rest of creation for anything, yet we and the rest of creation glorify him and bring him joy.

_____ God is the true God, and all his knowledge and words are both true and the final standard of truth.

_____ God does not have size or spatial dimensions and is present at every point of space with his whole being, yet God acts differently in different places.

4. Fill in the blanks of the three statements summarizing the biblical teaching on the Trinity.

God is _____ persons.
Each _____ is fully God.
There is ____ God.

5. True / False: There are no distinctions between the persons of the Trinity.

6. God created the universe out of:

   a. Matter
   b. Nothing
   c. Chaos
   d. Spirits

7. True / False: Humans are responsible for their actions.

8. Who is the mediator between us and God?

   a. A priest
   b. Our parents
   c. Angels
   d. Jesus Christ

9. True / False: Humans turn into angels when they die.

10. What does the name "Satan" mean?

   a. Prince of demons
   b. Adversary
   c. The serpent
   d. Evil angel

PART 3

The Doctrine of Man

CHAPTER 11

The Creation of Man

OPENING PRAYER

Lord, thank you for creating humanity in your image (Gen. 1:26). I am grateful for the privilege of being your created analogy and for the creation mandate to rule over and subdue the earth and to be fruitful and multiply. Help me to reflect your image in myself and see it in others more fully every day, and please help me to understand what it means to honor you with all of who you have made me to be, both physically and spiritually. Amen.

CHAPTER REVIEW

1. Why does Grudem advocate for the use of *man* to refer to all of humanity?

2. For what primary purpose did God create humans?

    a. He needed us

    b. For his glory

    c. He wanted to

    d. For our good

3. Fill in the blanks: Fullness of _____ is found in knowing God and delighting in the _____ of his character.

4. What does it mean to say that man is made in the "image of God"?

5. True / False: Humanity lost the image of God in the fall.

6. Describe how our redemption in Christ is related to the image of God.

7. When will the image of God be completely restored in believers?

    a. When they are saved
    b. When the Holy Spirit indwells them
    c. At Christ's return
    d. After the final judgment

8. Given each aspect of the image of God in humanity, define it briefly and then give an example:

9. Define the following terms:

   a. *Monism*:

   b. *Trichotomy*:

   c. *Dichotomy*:

10. Scripture uses what two words interchangeably?

   a. Mind and spirit
   b. Spirit and body
   c. Soul and spirit

BIBLICAL ENGAGEMENT

11. Read Genesis 1 and 2. What can you learn about the character of humanity through these two chapters?

12. After considering the scriptural evidence, which view of the essential nature of man do you think best accounts for the biblical data?

PERSONAL APPLICATION

13. How does the knowledge that you were created to glorify God make you feel? In what ways can you further live into this calling?

14. Does knowing that you are made in the image of God change the way you think about yourself? How so?

15. Does knowing that others are made in the image of God change the way you think about and relate to them? How so?

16. Do you tend to focus on the spiritual or the physical? How could holding to dichotomy with overall unity help you further understand your Christian growth?

CHAPTER 12

Man as Male and Female

OPENING PRAYER

Lord, thank you for your design of humanity as male and female. Satan hates the way you glorify yourself through humanity as male and female, and there is much confusion about this in our day. Show me the beauty of gender distinctions as well as the equality of dignity and worth they share. Help me to understand and love what it means to be the gender you created me to be. Amen.

CHAPTER REVIEW

1. In what three ways does the creation of man as male and female show God's image?

    a.

    b.

    c.

2. Where does interpersonal unity between men and women reach its full expression (in this age)?

    a. The church
    b. Family
    c. Marriage
    d. Parenthood

3. Fill in the blanks: If we are made equally in God's image, then certainly men and women are _____ important to God and equally _____ to him.

4. How do we see the equality of men and women on display at Pentecost?

5. Explain the relationship between the equality and distinction of the Trinity with the equality and distinction of men and women.

6. How did the fall and the subsequent curse affect male and female relationships?

7. How does Christ's redemption affect male and female relationships?

8. Compare and contrast the *egalitarian* and *complementarian* views on men and women.

BIBLICAL ENGAGEMENT

9. Read the account of the creation of man and woman in Genesis 1–2. Based on your reading of the text, what do you notice about men and women and their similarities and differences?

10. How does the New Testament differ from the Old Testament in how it teaches about male and female relationships?

PERSONAL APPLICATION

11. How has this chapter clarified or contradicted what you believe about gender?

12. Do you enjoy being your gender? Why or why not?

13. Can you truly say that you believe men and women are equally valuable in God's sight? How can you practice that belief in your actions going forward?

CHAPTER 13

Sin

OPENING PRAYER

Lord, help me to see my sin for what it is, a grievous attitude and act against you. Help me to seek forgiveness from you and recognize your grace and mercy. You are holy, and we have all rebelled against you, the Most High King. But you are gracious, and the Comforter you sent also kindly convicts of sin and brings us to godly sorrow and true repentance. As I study this chapter, please bring me to deeper sorrow for my sin so I can rest more deeply in the magnitude of your grace. Amen.

CHAPTER REVIEW

1. Define *sin*.

2. Fill in the blanks: A life that is _____ to God is one that has _____ purity not only in its _____, but also in its _____ of heart.

3. True / False: Our very nature is sinful.

4. Scripture defines sin in relationship to (circle all that apply):

    a. Humanity
    b. God's law
    c. Heaven
    d. God's moral character

5. Why must God hate sin?

6. True / False: Adam and Eve were the first beings to sin. Explain your answer.

7. What was the first human sin, and what three elements did it entail?

8. In what two ways do we inherit sin from Adam? Describe each.

a.

b.

9. True / False: Only part of our being is affected by sin.

10. Are there different degrees of sin? Explain your answer.

11. What happens when a Christian sins?

a. Our legal standing before God is changed
b. Our fellowship with God is disrupted
c. Our Christian life remains undamaged

12. True / False: There are people associated with the church that are not saved.

13. What is the unpardonable sin?

14. Why does God punish sin?

BIBLICAL ENGAGEMENT

15. Read Psalm 51. What characteristics of sin do we learn from this passage?

16. In Romans 5:12–21, what do you learn about the relationship between
Adam and Christ?

PERSONAL APPLICATION

17. Have you ever experienced deep sorrow for your sin? If not, how does
considering your sin feel now? If you have, where did that sorrow lead you?

18. In what ways do you tend to minimize, excuse, or rationalize your sin? In light of the teaching in this chapter, how can you adjust how you respond to your own sin coming to light?

19. The Bible says that although Christ knew no sin, he became sin for us (2 Cor. 5:21). In what ways are you walking in the freedom that comes from faith in him?

Part 3 Review Quiz

1. For what primary purpose did God create humans?

   a. He needed us
   b. For his glory
   c. He wanted to
   d. For our good

2. Being made in the image of God refers to:

   a. Being made in the exact likeness of God
   b. Man is like God and represents God
   c. Men are "little gods"

3. True / False: The image of God was lost in the fall.

4. Which of the following is not given as part of the essential nature of man according to Scripture?

   a. Body
   b. Mind
   c. Soul
   d. Spirit

5. True / False: Men and women are equal in value and personhood.

6. According to Grudem, distinctions in gender role:

   a. Were created good from the beginning
   b. Originated at the fall
   c. Do not exist
   d. Are a man-made fabrication

7. Fill in the blank: _____ is failure to conform to the moral law of God in act, attitude, or nature.

8. True / False: God is to be blamed for sin.

9. Which of the following did we inherit from Adam?

    a. Corruption
    b. Holiness
    c. Guilt
    d. Relationship with God

10. When a Christian sins:

    a. Nothing happens
    b. Their relationship with God is affected
    c. Their legal standing with God is changed
    d. They are condemned to hell

PART 4

The Doctrine of Christ

CHAPTER 14

The Person of Christ

OPENING PRAYER

Lord Jesus, you are the Way, the Truth, and the Life. As I study this chapter, please help me to know you more truly, depend on you more fully, and obey you more faithfully. You became the God-man, joyfully came to a world that hated you, and redeemed us from our lost and hopeless condition. Thank you for being our King and becoming a merciful and faithful high priest, meeting us where we were. I am forever grateful. Amen.

CHAPTER REVIEW

1. Fill in the blanks: Jesus Christ was _____ God and fully _____ in one _____, and will be so _____.

2. True / False: Jesus was born of a virgin.

3. How is the virgin birth related to inherited sin?

4. Jesus' thirst, tiredness, growth, hunger, and physical weakness point to:

    a. His sinlessness
    b. His masculinity
    c. His human body
    d. His deity

5. What emotions did Jesus experience during his life? List a few examples.

6. In what one respect was Jesus different from any other human in his humanity? Explain the importance of this.

7. Define *impeccable*. Do you think that Jesus was able to sin? Why or why not?

8. Jesus's humanity:

   a. Ended with his death
   b. Will remain until his return
   c. Will exist forever
   d. Never existed, he was and is only divine

9. Explain the different uses of the term *Lord* and how its use points to Christ's deity.

10. In what ways does Jesus display divine attributes?

11. Explain the *kenosis theory*.

12. True / False: It was not necessary for Jesus to be fully divine for our salvation. Explain.

13. Explain each of the following inadequate views of the person of Christ:

a. Apollinarianism

b. Nestorianism

c. Monophysitism (Eutychianism)

14. Explain how one nature of Christ does things that the other does not.

BIBLICAL ENGAGEMENT

15. Why did Jesus have to be fully human? Provide two to three reasons, with scriptural support.

16. Many claim that Jesus never claimed to be God. What scriptural evidence contradicts this claim?

PERSONAL APPLICATION

17. How does the fact that Jesus had a human body with weaknesses and limitations help you consider your own body?

18. Does knowing that Jesus obeyed God fully as a man help you as you consider your own temptation? How so?

19. Close your time in this chapter by writing a prayer of thanksgiving for the person of Christ.

CHAPTER 15

The Atonement

OPENING PRAYER

Lord Jesus, thank you for the work you have done on my behalf in your life and death to save me. You became one of us so you could save us from ourselves, our sin, and death. Thank you for your obedience in place of my disobedience, for bearing the wrath and death I deserved. Thank you for the cross and for laying down your life so I could live. Please help me to go much deeper in my understanding of the atonement as I study this chapter. Amen.

CHAPTER REVIEW

1. Define atonement:

2. What two attributes of God led to Christ coming to earth and dying for our sins?

    a. Love and wrath
    b. Justice and love
    c. Compassion and mercy
    d. Mercy and patience

3. True / False: It was necessary for God to save people.

4. Explain how God the Father is the primary emphasis and influence of Christ's work of redemption.

5. Why would forgiveness of sins not be sufficient in and of itself for meriting heaven?

6. What is the difference between Christ's active obedience and his passive obedience?

7. True / False: Christ only suffered for us on the cross. Explain your answer.

8. What does it mean that God imputed our sins to Christ?

9. Define *propitiation*:

10. Explain the term *penal substitution*.

11. Match the aspect of Christ's death with our need that we have as sinners.

a. Sacrifice   c. Reconciliation

b. Propitiation   d. Redemption

_____ We deserve to bear God's wrath against sin.

_____ We are in bondage to sin and to the kingdom of Satan.

_____ We deserve to die as the penalty for sin.

_____ We are separated from God by our sins.

BIBLICAL ENGAGEMENT

12. Read one of the gospel accounts of Jesus's death (Matt. 27:26–66; Mark 15:15–47; Luke 23:24–56; or John 19:16–42) while keeping in mind Grudem's explanation of the suffering involved in crucifixion. How does the knowledge of Christ's suffering on the cross on your behalf impact you?

PERSONAL APPLICATION

13. If you had to depend on your own record of obedience to merit heaven, how would you measure up? Thank God for his provision of Christ's perfect obedience on your behalf.

14. How does the knowledge of Christ's perfect life and sacrificial death on your behalf encourage you in your daily Christian walk?

CHAPTER 16

Resurrection and Ascension

OPENING PRAYER

Dear Lord, please help me to walk in the newness of life that is ours through the resurrection of Christ. Lead me to greater dependence on and confidence in him as my present mediator because he is the ascended Lord. Amen.

CHAPTER REVIEW

1. True / False: The Epistles depend upon the truth of a resurrected Christ.

2. How was Jesus's resurrection different from merely coming back from the dead?

3. In what ways was Jesus's resurrected body similar to our bodies now? In what ways is his resurrected body different from ours?

4. Fill in the blanks: The physical _____ of Jesus gives clear _____ of the goodness of the _____ creation that God originally made.

5. How does the resurrection of Christ relate to our own ability to live the Christian life?

6. What does the ascension of Christ refer to?

    a. Christ being put over all things
    b. Christ being lifted up into heaven
    c. Christ being lifted up on the cross
    d. Christ raising us from the dead

7. How does the ascension relate to the authority of Christ?

BIBLICAL ENGAGEMENT

8. Read John 11:1–44. What kinds of things do you learn about resurrection from this passage?

9. Now read one of the accounts of Jesus's resurrection from the gospels (Matt. 28:1–15; Mark 16:1–8; Luke 24:1–43 or John 20:1–29). How does Jesus' resurrection differ from Lazarus's?

PERSONAL APPLICATION

10. Does your church typically emphasize the death of Jesus or the resurrection of Jesus? How might an emphasis on one without the other minimize the power of the truth of the gospel?

11. How important is the resurrection of Christ in your daily life? What are ways that knowledge of the resurrection can help us as we go through tragedies, trials, and disappointments?

12. How does the ascension inform the way you think about your humanity, including your human body?

Part 4 Review Quiz

1. True / False: Jesus was born of a virgin.

2. Jesus had a body that:

    a. Seemed human
    b. Was divine
    c. Was human

3. Jesus was representative for us in his (circle all that apply):

    a. Obedience
    b. Divinity
    c. Sacrifice
    d. Sin

4. True / False: There is biblical evidence that Jesus is God.

5. Which two attributes of God are most related with the atonement?

    a. God's wrath and justice
    b. God's love and justice
    c. God's love and mercy
    d. God's mercy and grace

6. Match the aspect of Christ's death with our need that we have as sinners.

    a. Sacrifice
    b. Propitiation
    c. Reconciliation
    d. Redemption

_____ We deserve to bear God's wrath against sin.

_____ We are in bondage to sin and to the kingdom of Satan.

_____ We deserve to die as the penalty for sin.

_____ We are separated from God by our sins.

7. True / False: Jesus's resurrection was a new kind of life that had never been seen before.

8. Fill in the blank: After the resurrection, Jesus ascended into _____.

   a. The sky
   b. The spiritual world
   c. Heaven
   d. Hell

9. True / False: The Epistles depend upon the truth of a resurrected Christ.

10. Match each word with its definition below:

   a. Atonement
   b. Active obedience
   c. Passive obedience

_____ Christ's obedience of the law for his whole life on our behalf

_____ The work Christ did in his life and death to earn our salvation

_____ Christ's suffering and dying for our sins

The Doctrine of the Application of Redemption

CHAPTER 17

Common Grace

OPENING PRAYER

Lord, thank you that you are always revealing yourself and providing for your creation. Help me to be more aware of your common grace at work and have a heart filled with gratitude because of it. Amen.

CHAPTER REVIEW

1. Define *common grace*. Explain it in your own words.

2. Does God have two different kinds of grace? Explain.

3. How does the physical realm show evidence of God's common grace?

4. Fill in the blanks: All science and _____ carried out by non-Christians is a _____ of _____ grace.

5. How is God's common grace seen in the moral realm?

6. True / False: God does not ever answer the prayers of unbelievers.

7. Does common grace save people? Explain.

8. Draw a line between the evidence of grace and the kind of grace it points to:

Genuine repentance   Restraint from evil

Answered prayers   Purity of nature

True faith   Common grace

Rain for the harvest   Saving grace

9. What are the four reasons that God bestows common grace?

a.

b.

c.

d.

BIBLICAL ENGAGEMENT

10. Can you think of examples of common grace that are found in scripture? List them below. How do these examples help to broaden your understanding of the goodness of God?

PERSONAL APPLICATION

11. Have you ever thought about the concept of common grace before? How does understanding common grace help you see more fully God's activity in the world?

12. How can a proper understanding of common grace help you more fully and publicly praise God?

13. How will this doctrine change the way you interact with unbelievers around you?

CHAPTER 18

Election

OPENING PRAYER

Lord, I am grateful that you are the sovereign king of creation and that nothing happens outside your wise providence. Thank you for your sovereign grace that can never be earned. Help me to rest in your complete knowledge, goodness, and love. Amen.

CHAPTER REVIEW

1. Place in order and briefly define each of the following elements of "the order of salvation."

a.	Adoption	1.
b.	Conversion	2.
c.	Death	3.
d.	Election	4.
e.	Glorification	5.
f.	The gospel call	6.
g.	Justification	7.
h.	Perseverance	8.
i.	Regeneration	9.
j.	Sanctification	10.

2. Define *election*.

3. True / False: The doctrine of election is provided to instill fear in believers.

4. Explain how the doctrine of election encourages evangelism.

5. Fill in the blanks: When talking about our response to the _____ offer, Scripture continually views us not as mechanistic creatures or robots but as _____ _____, personal creatures who make willing choices to accept or reject the gospel.

6. What is meant by the term *knowing* when it is used in Scripture of God knowing his elect?

    a. Knowing facts about them
    b. Knowing them relationally
    c. Knowing their name
    d. Knowing what they will do in the future.

7. Grudem concludes that election is:

    a. Conditional
    b. Unconditional

8. What is the difference between libertarian free will (absolutely free will) and freedom of inclination?

9. True / False: It would be perfectly fair for God not to save anyone.

10. Define *reprobation*:

BIBLICAL ENGAGEMENT

11. List a few of the key passages relating to election and what each teaches us about this doctrine.

12. While discussing the passages that teach the doctrine of reprobation, Grudem mentions that we might wish that the Bible was written in another way. How can we respond to this feeling in a way that honors Scripture's authority?

PERSONAL APPLICATION

13. Why are you a Christian? What is the final reason God decided to save you?

14. Have you ever considered the doctrine of election as a reason to praise God? How has this chapter helped shape your understanding of this doctrine as a praiseworthy thing?

15. There are many portions of this doctrine that may cause discomfort for you. When you are faced with those feelings of discomfort, how do they change your attitude toward God and his Word? Ask God to teach you through his Spirit and his Word, even in areas of discomfort or confusion.

CHAPTER 19

The Gospel Call

OPENING PRAYER

Heavenly Father, thank you for taking the initiative in bringing your people to yourself through your sovereign grace. Help me to be a faithful witness for you, because no one is beyond your reach. Amen.

CHAPTER REVIEW

1. True / False: There is a definite order in which the blessings of salvation come to us.

2. Which member of the Trinity predestines people?

   a. The Father
   b. The Son
   c. The Holy Spirit

3. Fill in the blanks: Calling is a kind of _____ from the King of the universe, and it has such _____ that it brings about the _____ that it asks for in people's hearts.

4. Explain the difference between the *effective call* and the *gospel call*.

5. What are the three important elements of the gospel call?

    a.

    b.

    c.

6. True / False: It is not necessary to personally respond to the gospel call in order to be saved.

7. What two things are often mentioned together when the Bible speaks of conversion?

    a. Faith
    b. Works
    c. Repentance
    d. Obedience

8. How does the gospel call speak to human intellect, emotion, and will?

BIBLICAL ENGAGEMENT

9. Grudem makes clear in his discussion of Matthew 11:28–30 that these words are to be read as words that Jesus is speaking to each person, even now. What are some other words of Jesus that have this same kind of present-day implication and can be read just as personally as they were heard by the original audience?

10. Name some biblical examples of each of the elements of the gospel call. When these elements are present, how do the biblical hearers respond?

PERSONAL APPLICATION

11. Have you personally responded to the gospel call? If so, recount the time below. If not, let today be your day of salvation! Write a prayer asking Jesus to be Lord of your life and thank him for his salvation work on your behalf.

12. After reading about the importance of a personal response to the call of the gospel, how does that change how you think about the importance and value of evangelism?

CHAPTER 20

Regeneration

OPENING PRAYER

Dear Lord, I am deeply grateful that you have the power to bring those who are spiritually dead back to life and that you seek and save those who have turned their backs to you. Please help me to walk in the new life I have in Christ and faithfully share the good news with others who are walking in darkness. Amen.

CHAPTER REVIEW

1. Define *regeneration*.

2. True / False: We play an active role in the work of regeneration.

3. Which member(s) of the Trinity play a part in regeneration?

    a. God the Father
    b. God the Son
    c. God the Holy Spirit

4. Which comes first, regeneration or effective calling? Explain your answer.

5. True / False: Regeneration is a process. Explain your answer.

6. Why do some believe that regeneration comes after saving faith?

7. List some of the results of regeneration in the believer.

BIBLICAL ENGAGEMENT

8. Think about the analogy of birth used in regard to regeneration in John 1 and John 3. How is this a good analogy for this doctrine? Can you think of some other places in Scripture that use the analogy of birth?

9. Which passages give evidence for regeneration coming before saving faith? How have you seen evidence of that in your own life or the lives of others?

PERSONAL APPLICATION

10. How have you personally seen evidence of regeneration in your life? Thank the Lord for this work in you.

11. When you see evidence of regeneration in your life or in the lives of others, do you acknowledge it as a work of God? How can you grow in this act of worshipful acknowledgment?

CHAPTER 21

Conversion (Faith and Repentance)

OPENING PRAYER

Lord, thank you that when we turn from our sin and trust you instead of our useless self-effort, you give us a brand-new start and put us on the path of following in the steps of our Savior. Thank you for the saving power of the Spirit of holiness and the gospel of peace. Amen.

CHAPTER REVIEW

1. Define *conversion*.

2. Fill in the blanks: The turning from sin is called _____, and the turning to Christ is called _____.

3. True / False: Knowledge alone is enough for saving faith. Explain your answer.

4. Why does Grudem consider "trust" a more helpful word to use in discussing salvation rather than "faith" or "belief"?

5. List the three elements that must be present when a person comes to trust in Christ.

a.

b.

c.

6. Define *repentance.*

7. Repentance and faith are:

    a. Two different actions that happen at different times
    b. Completely unrelated
    c. Two sides of the same coin

8. Does repentance primarily mean "to change one's mind"? Explain your answer.

9. True / False: One must "pray the prayer" of salvation to be saved.

10. Do Christians outgrow the need for faith and repentance?

BIBLICAL ENGAGEMENT

11. Read 2 Corinthians 7:8–12. Describe the difference between worldly sorrow and godly grief. How does this relate to repentance?

PERSONAL APPLICATION

12. What role has repentance played in your faith life? Do you regularly walk in repentance and faith? How can you practice living a life filled with repentance and faith?

13. How does thinking about faith as trust help you consider your walk with the Lord? Do you regularly seek to know the Lord better in order to trust him more?

14. When sharing the gospel, how do you incorporate repentance into the gospel message?

CHAPTER 22

Justification and Adoption

OPENING PRAYER

Heavenly Father, you are the judge of all the earth. Thank you that I have been made right with you through the righteousness of Christ. Thank you that in him I will be able to stand before you, not only forgiven, but justified in your sight and adopted as your child. Please help me to rest in the security that comes with being your child, and give me a heart for the orphans in our world. In the name of Jesus, I pray. Amen.

CHAPTER REVIEW

1. Fill in the blanks: Justification comes _____ our faith and as God's _____ to our faith.

2. Define *justification*.

3. Explain the distinction between regeneration and justification.

4. Why is the forgiveness of sins insufficient for us to be in relationship with God?

5. Define *imputation*. In what other doctrines have we seen imputation discussed?

6. What is the primary difference between the Catholic and Protestant understandings of justification?

7. True / False: God was obligated to impute righteousness to his people.

8. Christians are justified:

    a. By the goodness of our faith
    b. By means of our faith
    c. By our works
    d. By earning merit with God

9. What meaning of the word *righteous* does James use? How is that different from Paul's use of the word?

10. Define *adoption*.

11. True / False: Our adoption only changes our relationship with God the Father, not with any other believers.

12. What witnesses to our adoption?

    a. Our faith
    b. The Holy Spirit
    c. Spiritual blessings
    d. A feeling of closeness

13. Is our adoption fully complete? Explain your answer.

BIBLICAL ENGAGEMENT

14. What biblical evidence points to justification being a legal act?

15. Read Romans 4. What evidence does Paul provide that we are justified by faith?

PERSONAL APPLICATION

16. How is it encouraging to know that the righteousness of Christ is imputed to us? How does understanding that reality change how you think about your Christian walk?

17. Reflect on the practical implications of justification by faith alone: hope and confidence. Do you see evidence of these in your life? If not, pray and ask God to increase your confidence in your justification by faith alone.

18. When you think of God as Father and yourself as an adopted child, how does that make you feel? Is it easy or hard to relate to God as Father? Why or why not?

CHAPTER 23

Sanctification
(Growth in Likeness to Christ)

OPENING PRAYER

Heavenly Father, thank you for the work of the Spirit in the lives of your people that makes us holy. I pray that I would be set apart more each day and that the fruit of the Spirit would flourish in my life. Amen.

CHAPTER REVIEW

1. Define *sanctification*.

2. What are some of the distinctions between justification and sanctification?

3. Name and briefly describe the three stages of sanctification.

a.

b.

c.

4. What two things can Christians not say regarding sin?

5. When is sanctification complete for our souls and bodies? Explain.

6. Describe the *perfectionist* position.

7. Fill in the blank: Sanctification should never stop _____ in this life.

8. Who participates in sanctification?

   a. Only God
   b. Only believers
   c. God and believers

9. What sort of role do believers play in sanctification?

10. True / False: Sanctification is only related to a person's spiritual life.

BIBLICAL ENGAGEMENT

11. Read 1 John and take notes regarding what it says about sin and sanctification.

PERSONAL APPLICATION

12. Did you notice in yourself a break from the ruling power and love of sin? Ask the Lord to help you increase your desire for holiness and decrease your desire to sin.

13. Do you find beauty and joy in your sanctification? Why or why not?

14. Chart your own sanctification process throughout your life. When did you have significant "high" points? What were some significant "low" points? Process these with the Lord in prayer.

CHAPTER 24

The Perseverance of the Saints (Remaining a Christian)

OPENING PRAYER

Sovereign King, thank you that you will complete the work you have begun in those you redeem. Help me to pursue holiness as one of your saints and, along the way, to rest in your sustaining grace. In Jesus's name I pray. Amen.

CHAPTER REVIEW

1. Define the *perseverance of the saints*.

2. What is the seal that the Lord has placed upon believers?

    a. The righteousness of Christ
    b. Their names written in the book of life
    c. The Holy Spirit
    d. Eternal life

3. Fill in the blanks: Believers' attainment of final salvation ultimately depends on _____ _____.

4. Why does Paul speak of the necessity of "continuing in the faith?"

5. What are some external signs of conversion that may or may not be signs of salvation?

6. What are the three questions a believer can ask themselves for real assurance?

a.

b.

c.

7. Can those who are convinced of the Arminian perspective ever have assurance of faith? Explain your answer.

BIBLICAL ENGAGEMENT

8. Which verses do you find most convincing in the argument for the perseverance of the saints?

9. What passages would you use to encourage someone who might be concerned about losing their faith?

PERSONAL APPLICATION

10. Have you ever feared "losing" your salvation? How does this chapter encourage you in your faith?

11. Ask yourself the three questions from question 6 above. Is the answer to any of these "no"? Pray and ask God to help you see evidence of his work in you.

CHAPTER 25

Death, the Intermediate State, and Glorification

OPENING PRAYER

Lord, thank you that death does not have the last word; Jesus does! Help me to grieve the death in this world as the result of our rebellion against you, and give me greater and greater hope that one day the dead in Christ will rise and that our bodies and souls will no longer be tragically separated. Thank you that Jesus had a physical body and that he rose bodily from the dead, and so will I! Help me to look forward to that day with great hope and live each day presenting myself, body and soul, to you as a living sacrifice. Amen.

CHAPTER REVIEW

1. True / False: Death is a punishment for Christians.

2. To what attribute of God does Grudem attribute the gradual bestowal of the benefits of Christ's redemptive work?

   a. Grace
   b. Wisdom
   c. Compassion
   d. Justice

3. How does suffering relate to God's discipline?

4. What is the appropriate response to the death of a Christian? What is the appropriate response to the death of an unbeliever?

5. Where does the doctrine of purgatory come from? What are some of the biblical arguments against it?

6. Describe "soul sleep." Why is this unbiblical?

7. Define *glorification*.

8. What will our resurrected bodies be like?

9. Fill in the blanks: When Christ _____, he will give us new resurrection _____ to be like his _____ body.

BIBLICAL ENGAGEMENT

10. List a few examples of deaths in Scripture. How was God glorified, even in the midst of these deaths?

11. What does 1 Corinthians 15:12–58 teach us about glorification or resurrection? Make a list of your findings.

PERSONAL APPLICATION

12. Are you willing to give up your own life for faithfulness to God? Why or why not? Ask God for the strength and conviction to be willing to give up all things for the sake of Christ.

13. If the resurrection were not true, how would that change your faith and your life?

14. How does the truth about bodily resurrection encourage you and provide you hope in the face of death?

Part 5 Review Quiz

1. Draw a line between the evidence of grace and the kind of grace it points to:

   Genuine repentance

   Answered prayers   Common grace

   True faith

   Rain for the harvest

   Restraint from evil   Saving grace

   Purity of nature

2. True / False: The doctrine of election is spoken of as an encouragement to evangelism.

3. The general gospel invitation:

   a. Goes to all people
   b. Is only for the elect

4. Genuine regeneration _____ bring results in life.

   a. Can
   b. Should
   c. Must
   d. Doesn't

5. True / False: Knowledge alone is sufficient for saving faith.

6. The idea of imputation is related to (circle all that apply):

    a. Guilt
    b. Creation
    c. Sin
    d. Righteousness

7. True / False: Sanctification is completed before the return of Christ.

8. What is the seal that the Lord has placed upon believers?

    a. The righteousness of Christ
    b. Their names written in the book of life
    c. The Holy Spirit
    d. Eternal life

9. True / False: Death is a punishment for Christians.

10. Match the following words with their definitions

    a. Election   e. Justification
    b. Effective calling   f. Adoption
    c. Regeneration   g. Sanctification
    d. Conversion

    _____ Our willing response to the gospel call, in which we sincerely repent of sins and place our trust in Christ for salvation.

    _____ An act of God before creation in which he chooses some people to be saved, not on account of any foreseen merit in them, but only because of his sovereign good pleasure.

    _____ An act of God whereby he makes us members of his family.

_____ An instantaneous legal act of God in which he (1) thinks of our sins as forgiven and Christ's righteousness as belonging to us, and (2) declares us to be righteous in his sight.

_____ A progressive work of God and man that makes us more and more free from sin and like Christ in our actual lives.

_____ A secret act of God in which he imparts new spiritual life to us.

_____ An act of God the Father, speaking through the human proclamation of the gospel, in which he summons people to himself in such a way that they respond in saving faith.

The Doctrine of the Church

CHAPTER 26

The Nature of the Church

OPENING PRAYER

Heavenly Father, thank you that you have created a people for yourself. As I learn about the church in this chapter, help me to increase my understanding about what the church is. As the husband of your people, you have promised that we will be pure and perfectly unified one day. Help me to love the church and seek after her growth in holiness and oneness. Amen.

CHAPTER REVIEW

1. What is the church? Write the definition in your own words. How is this definition different from how people commonly use the term *church* in the world today?

2. True / False: It is possible to know externally who is a true believer.

3. Explain the distinction between the invisible and the visible church.

4. True / False: The exact way in which biblical prophecies about the future will be fulfilled are difficult to decide with certainty.

5. How does Grudem describe the relationship between Israel and the church?

6. How does the kingdom of God relate to the church? What are the distinctions between the two?

7. The Reformation understanding of the marks of the true church are:

    a. Missions and evangelism
    b. Building and budget
    c. Word and sacrament
    d. Mission and vision

8. Fill in the blanks: The purity of the church is its degree of _____ from wrong doctrine and _____, and its degree of _____ to God's revealed _____ for the church.

9. Define *the unity of the church.*

10. What are some biblical and unbiblical reasons for separation in the church?

11. Briefly describe each of the three ministries related to the purpose of the church.

a.

b.

c.

BIBLICAL ENGAGEMENT

12. Is there a "church" in the Old Testament? Explain your answer using references to back up your points.

13. What sort of metaphors does the Bible use to describe the church? Pick a couple and explain them in more detail.

PERSONAL APPLICATION

14. How might you need to adjust how you think and speak about the church in light of the teaching in this chapter?

15. If you are a Christian, do you think you can say that you are living in a way that is striving to build up the church (1 Cor. 14:12) and seeking its purity and unity? Why or why not?

16. As you consider your own church, what characteristics of a true church are they excelling in? What areas might need growth? Consider how you can be a part of helping your church more fully live out these things.

CHAPTER 27

Baptism

OPENING PRAYER

Lord, thank you that by faith I have union with Christ and that I have died and been raised with him. Enable me to walk more fully in the complete identification with Christ that is displayed in my baptism. Please empower me to leave behind life in the flesh and to walk in the newness of life I have in Christ. In Jesus' name I pray. Amen.

CHAPTER REVIEW

1. Why do some protestants prefer the word *ordinance* over *sacrament*?

2. Define the "Baptistic" position that Grudem describes in this text. What is another name it is often called?

3. The mode of baptism in Scripture is:

    a. Sprinkling
    b. Watering
    c. Dropping
    d. Immersion

4. How does baptism relate to the death, burial, and resurrection of Christ?

5. Fill in the blank: Baptism is a _____ of beginning the Christian life.

6. What are the main differences between the Baptistic and the Catholic view on baptism?

7. Explain the covenant argument for paedobaptism.

8. What sort of benefit is baptism to those baptized?

9. True / False: Baptism is necessary for salvation.

BIBLICAL ENGAGEMENT

10. Read Romans 6:1–11 and Colossians 2:11–12. List the things you learn about baptism in these passages.

11. Having considered the Baptistic and paedobaptist views on baptism, which do you find most convincing based on the biblical evidence for each?

PERSONAL APPLICATION

12. Have you been baptized? Why or why not?

13. How significant do you think baptism is? If you had a Christian friend who had not been baptized, how would you counsel them?

14. Is baptism helpful for those that witness it? How so?

CHAPTER 28

The Lord's Supper

OPENING PRAYER

Dear Lord, I am profoundly grateful that Jesus took my punishment and died in my place. Thank you for the privilege of remembering this along with your people in the Lord's Supper. Every time I take it, please enable me to do it with the correct contrition and joy, and please help me to value the body of Christ more as we remember the body and blood together. Amen.

CHAPTER REVIEW

1. True / False: The Lord's Supper is one of two ordinances instituted by Jesus that are to be observed by the church.

2. When Christians participate in the Lord's Supper, they (circle all that apply):

    a. Give a clear sign of unity
    b. Remember that Jesus died for them
    c. Are saved
    d. Participate in the benefits of Jesus's death
    e. Receive spiritual nourishment

3. What are the two affirmations that Christ is making to us in the Lord's Supper?

    a.

    b.

4. Fill in the blank: When I take the Lord's Supper, I affirm my _____ in Christ.

5. Draw a line from the statement regarding the Lord's Supper to the view that believes it.

The elements become the body   Lutheran (Consubstantiation)
and blood of Christ.

The body of Christ is present "in,   Symbolic (Spiritual presence)
with, & under" the elements.

The elements symbolize the body   Catholic (Transubstantiation)
and blood of Christ.

6. Define *ex opere operato*. What does it refer to in this context?

7. What are Grudem's main critiques of the Roman Catholic teaching on the Lord's Supper?

8. Which of the three views do most protestants hold today?

    a. Catholic (transubstantiation)

    b. Lutheran (consubstantiation)

    c. Symbolic (spiritual presence)

9. Who should participate in the Lord's Supper?

10. Why is self-examination an aspect of participation in the Lord's Supper?

BIBLICAL ENGAGEMENT

11. Read the accounts of Jesus's institution of the Lord's Supper in all three synoptic gospels (Matt. 26:26–29; Mark 14:22–25; and Luke 22:14–20). How do these passages help inform your understanding of the importance and meaning of the Lord's Supper?

12. What are some Old Testament accounts of people eating and drinking in the presence of God? How do these provide a foundation for the Lord's Supper?

PERSONAL APPLICATION

13. Why do you think Jesus chose a meal to institute as a sacrament? How might you carry ideas from the Lord's Supper into your everyday meals?

14. Do you regularly partake in the sacrament of the Lord's Supper? Why or why not?

15. What view of the nature of Christ's presence in the Lord's Supper have you been taught in your church tradition? Do you think any differently after reading this chapter?

CHAPTER 29

Gifts of the Holy Spirit (I): General Questions

OPENING PRAYER

Lord, thank you for the sovereign grace of the Holy Spirit as he distributes his gifts to the church. I pray that I would seek the gifts of the Spirit for the good of the body of Christ and for your glory, not for my own exaltation. Amen.

CHAPTER REVIEW

1. Define *spiritual gift*.

2. When did the pouring out of the Holy Spirit occur?

    a. The Feast of Tabernacles

    b. Pentecost

    c. Passover

    d. Easter

3. Fill in the blanks: Spiritual gifts are given to _____ the church to carry out its _____ until Christ _____.

4. True / False: The Bible's lists of spiritual gifts are meant to be specific and exhaustive.

5. What does the phrase "in proportion to our faith" in Romans 12:6 imply about spiritual gifts?

6. Are all Christians expected to have the same gifts?

7. True / False: Spiritual gifts are always miraculous and otherworldly.

8. Who determines the distribution of gifts?

9. Summarize Grudem's explanation of the guidance of the Holy Spirit.

10. What are the four purposes of miracles that Grudem mentions?

a.

b.

c.

d.

11. True / False: Cessationists and charismatics don't need each other. Explain your answer.

BIBLICAL ENGAGEMENT

12. Name some examples of the Holy Spirit working in and through individuals in the Old Testament.

13. Name some examples of the Holy Spirit working in and through individuals in the New Testament.

14. What similarities and differences do you see between the two testaments?

PERSONAL APPLICATION

15. Before reading this chapter, how did you think about spiritual gifts? Has your understanding changed?

16. Are you aware of what spiritual gifts you have? How can you grow in your awareness and understanding of how the Lord has gifted you?

17. Have you ever seen or experienced any of the miraculous gifts of the Spirit? Which ones? Did you see them have a clearly edifying impact on others for the glory of God?

CHAPTER 30

Gifts of the Holy Spirit (II): Specific Gifts

OPENING PRAYER

Almighty God, I thank you for your miraculous power, and I'm grateful that you are still powerfully at work in and through the church. Give us discernment and wisdom to "test the spirits" (1 John 4:1) and to know if they are from you or not. I pray that we, your people, would be eager to see you work and eager for your kingdom to be advancing greatly in our day. Amen.

CHAPTER REVIEW

1. Define *prophecy*.

2. How was the word "prophet" used at the time of the New Testament?

3. True / False: There is one prophet in every church.

4. How does Grudem say that we should consider the words of prophets today?

    a. As human words
    b. As divine words
    c. Equal in authority with scripture
    d. Infallible

5. Define *revelation* as Grudem describes Paul using it in 1 Corinthians 14:30–31.

6. True / False: God communicates directly with individuals.

7. Describe the distinction between prophecy and teaching.

8. Fill in the blanks: The gift of teaching in the New Testament is the _____ to explain Scripture and _____ it to people's lives.

9. True / False: Physical sickness is a result of the fall.

10. What is a helpful way for Christians view the use of medicine?

11. Should Christians pray for healing? Explain your answer.

12. What word does Grudem argue tongues should be translated as?

    a. Angelic
    b. Miraculous
    c. Languages
    d. Voice

13. Define *speaking in tongues.*

14. True / False: Speaking in tongues only refers to the use of human languages.

BIBLICAL ENGAGEMENT

15. Compare and contrast prophecy in the Old Testament and prophecy in the New Testament. Include references where possible.

16. What can we learn about healing from Jesus' life and example?

PERSONAL APPLICATION

17. Do you come from a continuationist or cessationist background? Has this chapter changed your mind on anything you used to think?

18. Do you regularly pray for healing for yourself and others? How do you respond when there is healing? How do you respond when there isn't healing?

19. Which of these gifts do you think your church needs or needs more of? How could you respond to this need in a helpful manner?

Part 6 Review Quiz

1. The church is:

    a. Visible
    b. Invisible
    c. Both a and b

2. True / False: There are true churches and false churches.

3. In the Bible, baptism was done by:

    a. Sprinkling
    b. Immersion
    c. We don't know

4. True / False: Baptism is necessary for salvation.

5. Who should participate in the Lord's Supper?

    a. Anyone who wants to
    b. Only believers
    c. Only baptized believers
    d. Only members of the church

6. Transubstantiation argues that:

    a. The bread and wine symbolize Christ's body and blood.
    b. The bread and wine become Christ's body and blood.
    c. Christ's body and blood are in, with, and under the bread and wine.

7. True / False: Spiritual gifts are always miraculous and otherworldly.

8. True / False: God communicates directly with individuals.

9. What word does Grudem argue tongues should be translated as?

    a. Angelic
    b. Miraculous
    c. Languages
    d. Voice

10. Match the following words to their definition below:

    a. Church   d. Teaching
    b. Spiritual gift   e. Tongues
    c. Prophecy   f. Healing

_____ God granting a partial foretaste of the perfect health that will be ours for eternity

_____ Any ability that is empowered by the Holy Spirit and used in any ministry of the church

_____ Telling something that God has spontaneously brought to mind

_____ The community of all true believers for all time

_____ The ability to explain Scripture and apply it to people's lives

_____ Prayer or praise spoken in syllables not understood by the speaker

PART 7

The Doctrine
of the Future

CHAPTER 31

The Return of Christ: When and How?

OPENING PRAYER

Lord, thank you for the blessed hope of Christ's return. Please enable me to live my whole life in light of his second coming. Fill my soul with hope and longing to see him when the dead in Christ shall rise with him. *Maranatha!* Amen.

CHAPTER REVIEW

1. Define *eschatology*.

2. Fill in the blanks: The return of Christ will be sudden, _____, visible, and _____.

3. How should we await Christ's return?

    a. With fear
    b. With eager longing
    c. With curiosity
    d. With resignation

4. True / False: Since the return of Christ is imminent, we should not engage in long-term activities.

5. How would the biblical authors respond to someone who claimed to know exactly when Christ would return?

6. What are the six signs that the Bible says must happen before Christ returns?

a.

b.

c.

d.

e.

f.

7. How does Grudem reconcile both that we should be prepared for Christ's imminent return and that there are certain signs that will precede it?

8. Define *preterism.*

BIBLICAL ENGAGEMENT

9. How would you respond biblically to those who claim to know when Christ will return? What passages would you point them to?

10. List a few Bible verses that support each of the four characteristics of the return of Christ (sudden, personal, visible, and bodily).

PERSONAL APPLICATION

11. Do you long for Jesus to return? If so, what in your experiences and thinking have led to that longing? If not, what do you think may be missing from your perspective?

12. What are ways that we should practically "be ready" for Christ's return? How can you put practices into your life that can help you live this out?

CHAPTER 32

The Millennium

OPENING PRAYER

King of Kings, I thank you that the day is coming when your will will forever be done on earth as it is in heaven. This is your world—you made it and are remaking it and redeeming it. I look forward to the day when Jesus will reign once and for all, vanquish the powers of darkness, and put an end to sin and death. Amen.

CHAPTER REVIEW

1. What does the word *millennium* mean?

    a. One million years
    b. One year
    c. One hundred years
    d. One thousand years

2. Briefly describe each of the three major views on the time and nature of the millennium.

Amillennialism

Postmillennialism

Premillennialism

3. True / False: The amillennial view teaches that Jesus will not return until after the secret rapture of God's people.

4. What are the differences between the classical premillennial view and the dispensational premillennial view?

5. Which view is Grudem a proponent of and why?

6. Fill in the blanks: The "pretribulation rapture" view holds that when Christ _____ returns, the church will be _____ into _____ to be with him.

BIBLICAL ENGAGEMENT

7. Read Revelation 20:1–6. Which of the three views described in this chapter do you think best accounts for this passage and the rest of biblical teaching? What are the strengths and weaknesses of the view that you chose?

PERSONAL APPLICATION

8. What view did you hold of the millennium before you read this chapter, if any? How has your view changed, if at all?

9. How does your view on the millennium change the way you live your Christian life?

10. Do you long for the kingdom of God to be established on earth? In what ways do you pray and seek to bring about realities of the kingdom even before it arrives fully?

CHAPTER 33

The Final Judgment and Eternal Punishment

OPENING PRAYER

Judge of the earth, I am grateful that your perfect justice will one day be poured out, and all the wrongs of human history will be made right. Thank you that Jesus was judged in my place so I do not need to fear that day. Please give me boldness in warning people to flee the wrath to come and find freedom from eternal punishment in Christ. Amen.

CHAPTER REVIEW

1. Fill in the blank: The final judgement is the _____ of many precursors in which God rewarded righteousness or punished unrighteousness throughout history.

2. When will the final judgment occur?

   a. Before the rebellion
   b. When evil reaches its maximum
   c. After the millennium
   d. The Bible doesn't say

3. What implies that there will be degrees of punishment and degrees of reward?

4. True / False: Believers, unbelievers, and angels will all face a final judgment.

5. Why is a final judgment necessary?

6. Briefly summarize the four moral applications Grudem gives for the final judgment.

    a.

    b.

    c.

    d.

7. Define *hell*.

8. Describe the view of *annihilationism*.

9. True / False: If God were not to execute eternal punishment, his justice would not be satisfied and his glory would not be furthered in the way he deems wise.

BIBLICAL ENGAGEMENT

10. Provide three scriptural evidences for the final judgment. What do these passages teach regarding the judgment?

PERSONAL APPLICATION

11. What is your initial emotional reaction when you hear about the final judgement and eternal punishment? Has this chapter changed your perspective?

12. Does the doctrine of final judgment help you to be more able to forgive others? Why or why not?

13. Do you often think about Jesus as the coming judge of the world? How should thinking of Jesus as the judge of all the earth increase your trust in and healthy fear of him?

CHAPTER 34

The New Heavens and New Earth

OPENING PRAYER

Lord, I long for the day when sin will be no more, and you will wipe away every tear and defeat sin and Satan and bring your work in redemptive history to a glorious consummation. Help me live every day looking forward to that great day when your people from every tongue and tribe and nation gather around your throne, praising your name forever. In the name of the Father, Son, and Holy Spirit I pray. Amen.

CHAPTER REVIEW

1. True / False: The Bible teaches that believers will live with God in heaven forever and the earth will be no more.

2. Define *heaven*.

3. Fill in the blanks: The _____ creation will be renewed, and we will continue to _____ and act in it.

4. In the new heavens and the new earth, we will:

   a. Live in a disembodied state
   b. Live in resurrected bodies
   c. Live a life totally unlike our own

5. Will we know God fully in the new heavens and the new earth? Explain your answer.

6. Fill in the blanks: The new _____ will be a place of great _____ and abundance and _____ in the presence of _____.

7. True / False: When we finally see the Lord face-to-face, our hearts will want nothing else.

BIBLICAL ENGAGEMENT

8. What is the biblical evidence that heaven is a place?

PERSONAL APPLICATION

9. How did this chapter increase your understanding of the new heavens and the new earth?

10. Does the idea that we will work, play, eat, create, and enjoy life in many ways that are similar to how we experience life now increase your desire for heaven? How so?

11. Is life *with* God a chief desire of yours? Why or why not?

12. How would your daily life be affected if you had an increased desire for the life to come? Pray and ask God for this desire to grow in you.

Part 7 Review Quiz

1. What is the study of future events often called?

   a. Future study
   b. Eschatology
   c. Endology

2. True / False: Jesus will return suddenly, personally, visibly, and bodily.

3. How should we await Christ's return?

   a. With fear
   b. With eager longing
   c. With curiosity
   d. With resignation

4. What does the word *millennium* mean?

   a. One million years
   b. One year
   c. One hundred years
   d. One thousand years

5. Match the following statements with the corresponding belief about the millennium:

   a. Amillennialism
   b. Postmillennialism
   c. Premillennialism

_____ There will be no future millennium

_____ Believers will reign with Christ on earth

_____ Christ will return after the millennium

_____ The present church age will continue until Christ's return

_____ Christ will come back before the millennium

_____ A "millennial age" of peace and righteousness on earth will occur before Christ's return

_____ All of the end-time events will happen immediately after Christ's return

_____ After the tribulation at the end of the church age, Christ will return to establish a millennial kingdom

_____ Optimism about the power of the gospel to bring about much good in the world

6. Who will be the judge at the final judgment?

    a. Jesus
    b. The Father
    c. The Holy Spirit

7. True / False: Believers, unbelievers, and angels will all face a final judgment.

8. True / False: If God were not to execute eternal punishment, his justice would not be satisfied and his glory would not be furthered in the way he deems wise.

9. In the new heavens and the new earth, we will:

    a. Live in a disembodied state
    b. Live in resurrected bodies
    c. Live a life totally unlike our own

10. True / False: When we finally see the Lord face-to-fact, our hearts will want nothing else.

Printed in the USA
CPSIA information can be obtained
at www.ICGtesting.com
JSHW011205131124
73541JS00002B/2